WHERE'S THE PAIR?

a spotting book

Britta Teckentrup

Down from a fir tree,
a birdie descends,
joining a flock
of feathery friends.

Stretching their wings out
and tweeting together,
which of the flock
are birds of a feather?

Clever chameleons
change colour all day
from blue, green and yellow
to black, brown and grey.

As they bask in the heat
of a warm sunny patch,
which sleepy lizards
perfectly match?

Up in the meadow
lives a herd of yaks,
munching on grass
and warming their backs.

With their handlebar horns
they all look like trouble!
Can you discover
the yak with a double?

A kennel of dogs
takes a walk in the park.
Getting excited,
one starts to bark.

Yapping and howling,
they cause quite a stir.
Can you spot the pair
with the very same fur?

A gang of cool cats
on soft, padded paws,
can pounce like tigers –
watch out for those claws!

But give them a stroke
and these felines will purr!
Which two cats match,
both collar and fur?

An army of frogs,
of all shapes and sizes
in a hopping contest
would win all the prizes!

As they play leapfrog,
their favourite game,
can you see two frogs
exactly the same?

These glittery fish
with their rainbow of scales,
dart through the water,
swishing their tails.

Twisting and turning,
this shoal loves to play.
Which pair are heading
in the wrong way?

Buzzing dragonflies
glint in the light,
their flashing wings,
shining so bright.

As they skim and swoop,
which pair can you spy,
flying so gracefully
up in the sky?

A sloth of brown bears
march to and fro,
all dressed up
with nowhere to go!

Look very closely
and try to find
two grizzly bears
of the very same kind!

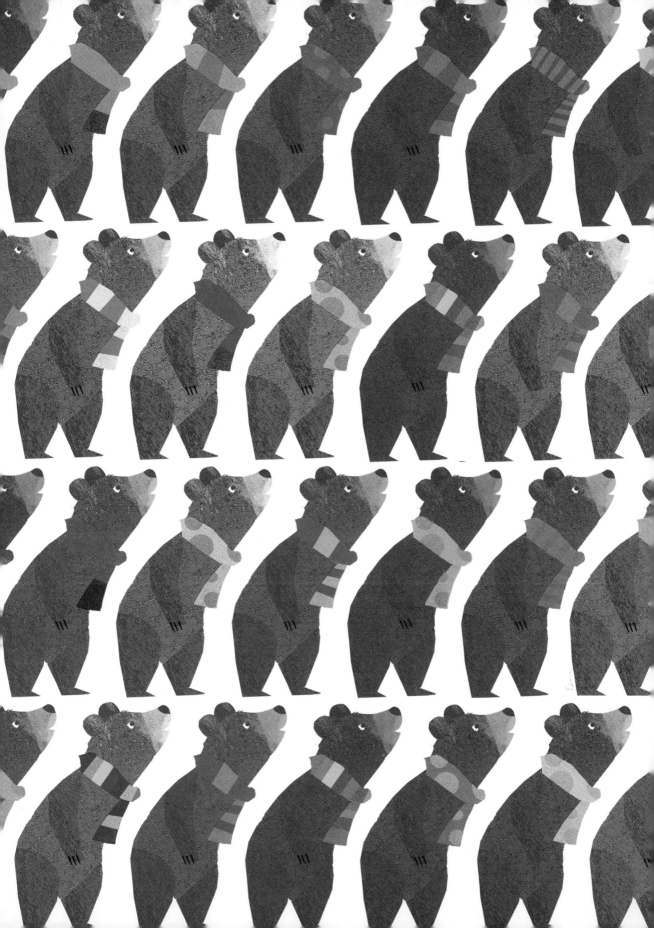

A scurry of squirrels
playing together,
search high and low
for their stores of treasure!

Not every squirrel
has found a treat.
Where is the pair
with no acorn to eat?

A dazzle of zebras,
each one black and white,
are camouflaged well
by their stripes dark and light.

Although all their patterns
are similar types,
which two are sporting
identical stripes?

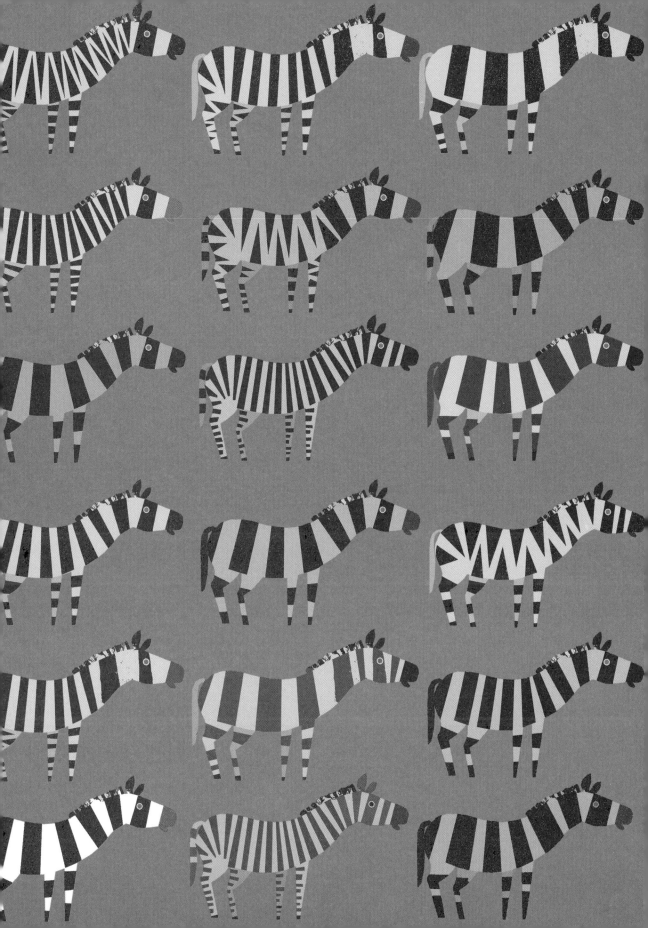

A romp of otters
gather to play,
diving and swimming
and splashing all day.

Now it's time for tea
and their favourite dish!
Which matching otters
have caught a fish?

Toucan acrobats
stand in a row;
their balancing act
is the best in the show.

It's hard to keep still
in the very same spot.
Which is the pair
amongst the flock?

The beetles are busy
day in, day out;
in their colourful armour
they scuttle about.

They're tricky to spot
but can you see where
two little beetles
make one perfect pair?

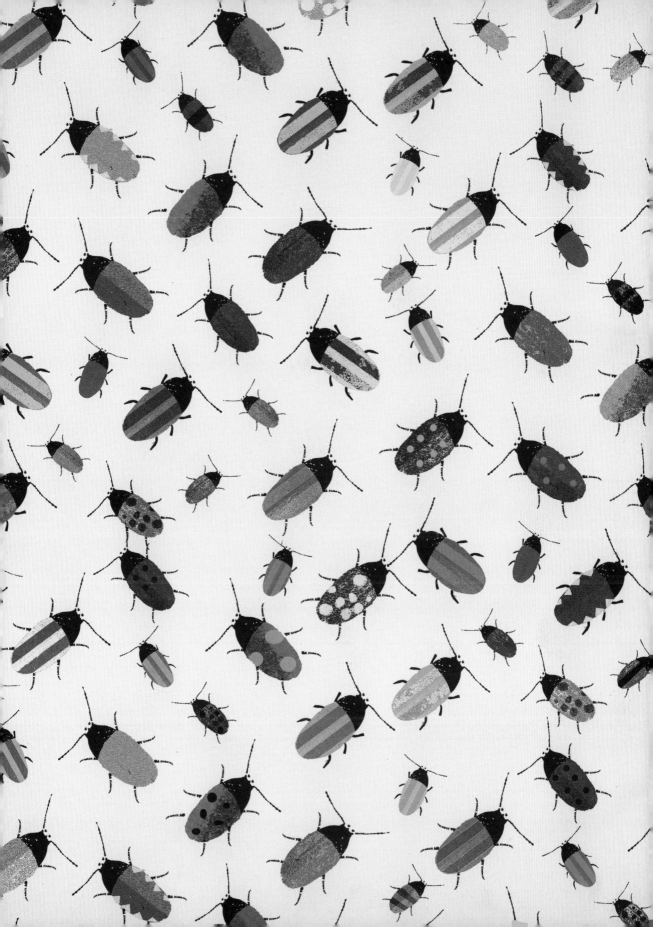

These charming creatures
come back two by two
to croak, bark and mieow
a 'goodbye' to you.

But now a last challenge:
dotted here and there
are just five sets of twins
that make a real pair!

BIG PICTURE PRESS

www.bigpicturepress.net

First published in the UK and Australia in 2015 by Big Picture Press,
part of the Bonnier Publishing Group,
The Plaza, 535 King's Road, London, SW10 0SZ
www.bonnierpublishing.com

5 7 9 10 8 6

ISBN 978-1-78370-169-8

Printed in China

This book was typeset in Brown.
The illustrations were created digitally.

Edited by Alison Ritchie
Designed by Andy Mansfield